The Limitless Mind: Learn to Reach Your Full Potential through Self-Talk and Positive Affirmations

Disclaimer and Terms of Use: Effort has been made to ensure that the information in this book is accurate and complete, however, the author and the publisher do not warrant the accuracy of the information, text and graphics contained within the book due to the rapidly changing nature of science, research, known and unknown facts and internet. The Author and the publisher do not hold any responsibility for errors, omissions or contrary interpretation of the subject matter herein. This book is presented solely for motivational and informational purposes only.

Summary

Many people now realize the power of positive affirmations and the fact that everyone holds his or her destiny in their own hands. This is why the topic of self-talk is getting a lot of attention because it has importance in various aspects of life such as work, relationships and so on. This book serves as a guide to take you through the journey of practicing positive affirmations.

It begins by showing you the power of positive affirmations and what you stand to gain from them. You might know their benefits and have an interest in enjoying this power but do not have an idea of how to go about it. Don't worry because the book tackles the steps you can follow to incorporate positive affirmations in your daily life. There are times when you might have the desire to be positive but your inner critic voice won't give you a chance therefore thwarting your efforts of thinking positively. When this happens, you need to know how to shut out those negative feelings and this book provides you with the tips you can apply in order to do that. With this information, you are able to engage in positive affirmations that can change your life.

Table of Contents

Disclaimer   1

Summary   3

Introduction 5

Chapter 1: Benefits of Positive Affirmations 6

Chapter 2: How you can use positive affirmations effectively   12

Chapter 3: Tips for successfully applying positive affirmations 22

Chapter 4: How you can silence inner critic   26

Chapter 5: Steps towards achieving positive self-talk   34

Final thoughts   45

Introduction

There is a lot of talk about positive affirmations that may make you wonder what the big deal is. First of all, it is really a big deal because how you think of yourself plays a major role in the kind of experiences you will have. Positive affirmations are important in helping us shape our fate in various ways with regards to dreams, imaginations and expectations. The level of happiness we achieve in life is determined by how we think about ourselves.

Research shows that having positive thoughts result in benefits that are both short term and long term. Therefore, if you are in a situation where you have to choose between positive and negative thoughts, why not opt for the former and enjoy these benefits? This is what people mean when they talk of seeing a glass as half full as opposed to half empty. When you think about it, the level of water is the same in the glass but the difference lies in how the different people view it.

Positive affirmations refer to thoughts and sayings that you say to yourself whether it is quietly inside your head or loudly. The role of positive affirmations is to boost your mind, body and soul. You can try them out the next time you have negative thoughts or you make a mistake.

Positive affirmations or what we refer to as the self-talk have lots of benefits which you can enjoy. There are so many challenges and stresses we face in our daily life that can bring us down. These make us think negatively about most things in life. You might end up thinking that you are not good enough based on the failures you have experienced in life. At times we resort to making negative statements about ourselves when we get criticized by our superiors, friends or family. In the end, this kind of negativity damages our self-esteem and it can even reach extreme cases if not handled in time. This is something we shouldn't subject ourselves too since we have the power to control our thoughts and dictate our destiny. Knowing the benefits of positive affirmations can give you the motivation to get started on practising them. One of the best things about positive affirmation is the fact that you are not the only one who benefits from them even if you are the one putting them in action; they rub off on the people you interact with too.

1. Stronger muscles

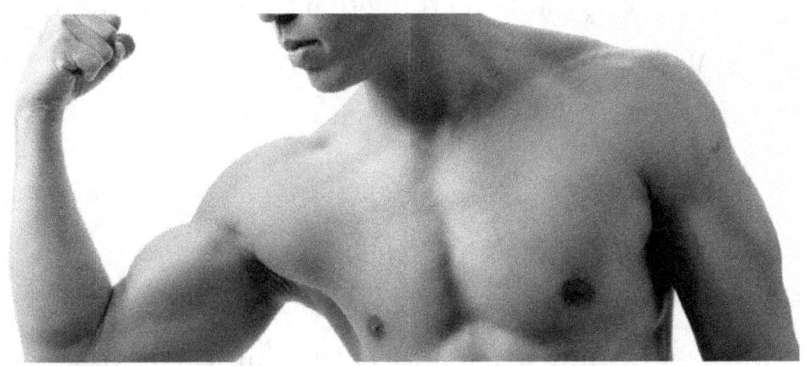

This is one of the benefits that many people do not know about. Studies carried out confirmed that people who continuously use positive words and thoughts have stronger muscles compared to those who don't or to those with negative thoughts and feelings. If you thought that hitting the gym was the only way to strengthen your muscles then you are wrong. According to research, the act of filling your subconscious with positive words serves to strengthen your muscles and make them more active. On the other hand, your muscles tend to get weak when you think and talk of being tired or complain about something.

2. It boost one's capabilities, talents and skills

Self talk can help your strengths and capabilities manifest themselves. When you constantly remind yourself of your capabilities and do not hesitate to pursue your goals in life then you have a higher chance of getting positive results. If you look at successful people, most of them usually have smiles on their faces, a brighter outlook on life and have a worry-free air around them. This is the same thing that positive affirmations can do to you. Self-talk is guided by the principle that your mind is very powerful to an extent that it wills your body to follow what it says.

There are people who believe that self-talk can lead to some mysterious effects that cannot be explained even by intellectuals. According to experts, positive affirmations are able to penetrate your subconscious therefore affecting your attitude, how you act or behave.

3. Increased energy level

Self talk has the ability to affect your energy levels too. When you think about it, you will notice that people who normally have positive thoughts are happy most of the time. This is possible because positive affirmation has an effect on both the physical and emotional well-being of someone. This is why experts stress that you need to begin your day on a positive note in order for the rest of the day to be great too. This good energy can spread to the various parts of your life.

4. Enhances your creativity

Successful people are normally creative because they are always looking for better ways of accomplishing their goals or of gaining more success with their already accomplished goals. We have something in our brains known as the Reticular Activating System (RAS) which acts like a filter therefore allowing the information we require and doing away with those we don't. When you repeat an affirmation then there are a variety of things that take place. One of them is that it informs your RAS that what you are saying is important to you. After this happens, the RAS becomes busy trying to see the various ways in which it can be possible for you to achieve your goals. In case you want to shed some pounds and achieve your ideal weight then you will start noticing almost every gym around you or the various weight loss products you hadn't paid attention to before. In case you want to acquire more money then you will be more aware of investment and earning opportunities. Generally, affirmation will make your creativity to show and you will find various ways of achieving your goals.

What you have to know about positive affirmations is that, you have to do the positive self-talk over and over again. This is the engine your body needs to be able to move forward. When debating on whether or not to engage in positive self-talk, always remember that it is necessary to clearly affirm any goal or vision you may have in order to make them come true. One trick you should learn about positive affirmations is that they work better when you refer to them in the present tense. Experts claim that time is of the essence in effecting change and so and the present tense emphasizes the time which is now and not tomorrow.

Chapter 2: How you can use positive affirmations effectively

Making positive statements about yourself is important in helping your subconscious mind create a positive perception of yourself. Affirmations can help you alter harmful behaviors you have and this will push you closer to your goals. In addition to that, you can use them to get rid of the damage done by negative thoughts and statements overtime. Although it is easier to come up with positive affirmations, dedication is required to be able to practice these affirmations.

According to experts, the first prerequisite for success is knowing what you want. In order for affirmations to be effective, they must originate from you so don't wait for other people to give you those affirmations. What you think about yourself is what matters most in this case. If other people share those opinions then it will just be a bonus for you.

1. **Decide on the content**

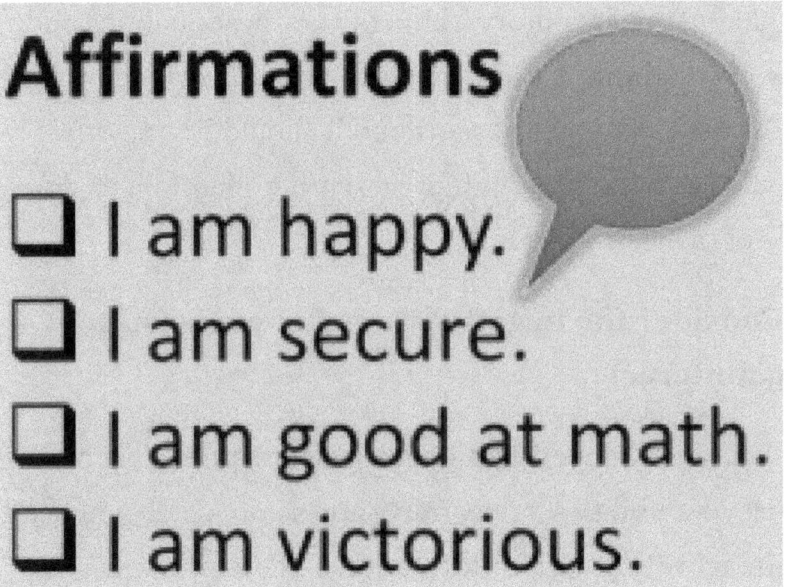

Before you start making affirmations about yourself, it is important to decide on what you want to say. Most of the times, we put emphasis on the things we don't appreciate about ourselves and those we would like to change if given the chance. You can start focusing on what you really like about yourself in order to use self-talk to effect change. Keeping an inventory is essential in this process because it will serve as a reminder of all the good things you can say about yourself which will help you break the cycle of negative thoughts and statements. You will be able to appreciate yourself more when you see a significantly long list of good things about you. This will make it easier to accept the positive affirmations you give yourself.

When making this inventory, think of your best qualities and abilities. If you think you are gorgeous or hardworking, write it down. Let each sentence be short and it should begin with "I" and should be in the present tense as earlier mentioned. An example of this is "I am gorgeous".

2. Consider the negative thoughts you want to counteract

You may have developed some negative perceptions of yourself regarding your abilities, appearance and so on which you need to counteract with positive affirmations. These positive affirmations meant for counteracting the negative ones are normally known as counter-scripts. It helps to come up with a list of the unhealthy self- perceptions that you would like to change. You can then attach them to the specific goals you aim at achieving and an example is quitting smoking.

3. Make priorities of the things you want to work on

You may be surprised at the many goals you want to accomplish or several counter-scripts you require. However, the best thing to do is focus on few affirmations at a given time. You can therefore make your list beginning with the most urgent or important and dealing with them first. After accomplishing those goals or seeing some improvements in the various areas chosen, you can come up with new affirmations. Although it is possible to begin by using many affirmations at once, it is advisable to stick to five or less at a given time.

4. Write your affirmations

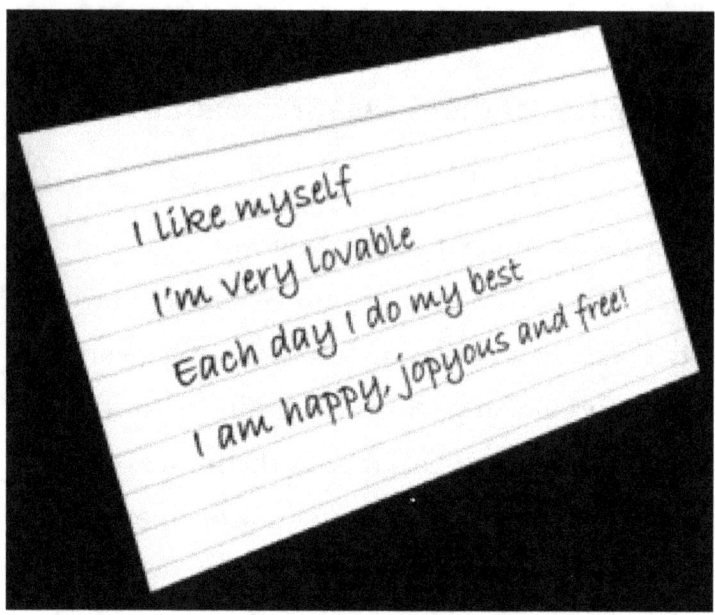

Initially, you wrote your affirmations based on the positive attributes you currently have of yourself. These can be used as counter-scripts individually or they can be combined with other affirmations meant to determine your future behavior. The affirmations you need to influence future behavior must have the same basis as the previous ones in the sense that they should also begin with "I" and should be short, clear and straight to the point. Affirmations aimed at accomplishing future goals can be divided in to two;

- Statements that start with " I can" are meant to make you feel like you can achieve your goals. A good example is if you are thinking of quitting smoking then you can say "I can quit smoking."According to experts, you should avoid adding anything negative to these statements and so other ways you can use to enforce the same positive affirmation includes "I can become smoke-free."

- There are statements that begin with "I will." You can create positive self-talk with these statements implying that you will put to use the ability you have to achieve your goal. Therefore, your statement in this case can be "I will be smoke-free today." You can also say "I will smoke less today." In this case too, make sure the affirmations have a positive tone to them and should talk about what you intend to do on that particular day to push you closer to your long-term goal.

5. **Match your positive qualities with your goals**

I give myself permission to be happy

You listed some positive attributes you have in the initial step and it is time to look at those qualities and try to determine the ones that can propel you towards achieving the set goals. For example, if your goal is to quit smoking then you require courage or will- power to be able to do it. Go through your initial list or reflect on your qualities and see if you have courage. In case courage is not among your strong qualities but you have beauty then you may focus on quitting smoking in order to maintain that beauty. If you care about your family then this thought can push you to quit smoking in order to be there for them and set a good example. About two to three positive affirmations are sufficient to work hand in hand with the affirmation concerning the goals you want to achieve.

6. Make your affirmations visible

If you want your affirmations to be effective then you need to repeat them. Try to think about your affirmations several times daily and by doing this; it will be easier to apply them. There are various ways of doing this;

- Be committed to writing down your affirmations in your diary or journal every morning and every night before you sleep.

You can then say these affirmations many times a day. The idea is to have your affirmation in your mind the minute you wake up and to be the last thought on your mind before you sleep.

- Meditate on those affirmations.

Sometimes you need to shut the rest of the world out and just have some private time with your affirmations. Close your eyes, say the words of affirmation and repeat them. You can then think about these affirmations and the meaning they hold to you. Try to visualize the future using your affirmations and allow yourself to feel the emotions arising from them.

- It is important to put reminders in different places where you can see them. Sticky notes or index cards are great for doing this and you can create several cards for every affirmation. For example, you can put some cards at the spot you normally relax at the kitchen table, while you can tape another one on your car's steering wheel.

When you go to the office, you can put another card inside your desk drawer or even stick it on your computer monitor and so on. The idea is to always think about your affirmations. Whenever you see a card with an affirmation on it, you need to read it and then think about its meaning. It is advisable to carry your affirmation with you. You can create a list of these affirmations which you can carry inside your wallet or purse. These will come in handy when you are about to go off-track from your goals because you will be able to read them and remind yourself of the bigger picture.

7. **Continue using your affirmations**

Although the process of using positive affirmations is a big one, there are many who give up halfway through it. In order for something to firmly stick in your mind, you need to affirm it again and again. Therefore, the more you use your affirmations, the higher the chances of your mind accepting them and the higher the chances of accomplishing them too.

Chapter 3: Tips for successfully applying positive affirmations

Positive affirmations contain great power as explained earlier on. However, there are some tips you can apply to help make the transition to positive thinking easier and successful.

- It is important to connect positive affirmations to your emotions. When you get these emotions, think of how you will feel when you finally achieve your goals. If it isn't a goal you have in mind then you can just revel in the feeling of knowing that there is something you are good at. Affirmations cannot be powerful on their own but when combined with emotions then anything is possible.

- One of the things you can do is make your password one of your affirmations or the affirmation you are currently focusing on. This means you will have to use it frequently to enable it stick in your mind therefore becoming part of you.
- Use affirmations together with visualizations. Visualizing your affirmations help to make them more real and so you should use the two together in order to make the process more effective. When doing this, ensure you add some mental visualization involving as many senses as you can such as smell, touch and sight among others.
- Involve your friends in declaring your affirmations. Self –affirmations are the best form of affirmation due to the fact that they free you from relying on other people for approval. However, getting affirmations from others also serve to give you more self confidence in the same way that negative scripts can harm you. You can ask your friends to help you in this journey by verbalizing a few of your affirmations. An example is if a friend tells you that he has noticed you eating very healthy meals of late and goes on to say that it must give you a great feeling. This will make you feel good about eating healthy and will motivate you to keep at it.
- Keep your reminders in discreet places.

There are issues you might be struggling with and you might be practicing positive affirmations in these areas although you may not want everyone to know about them. If this is the case then you can keep your reminders in discreet places. However, do not forget that you need to see these reminders often. Therefore, think of a place that is discreet but will still enable your reminders to perform their role.

- There are times when it may be hard to truly believe in particular affirmations and in these cases, it helps to try using the words "I choose" when making your affirmations. You can use them to help yourself achieve your goals. For example, you can say "I choose to maintain a healthy weight."

- Try recording your affirmations. It may not be very clear whether you believe in your affirmations when you are actually saying them. Recording them and playing the recording can help you figure out if you have enough conviction in your voice. If you don't sound convincing to yourself then it means you need to work harder at it and this will help you succeed with time.

MY WORDS ARE POWERFUL

Positive thoughts and affirmations are important for you to achieve happiness and success in various areas of your life. This doesn't mean that self-criticism is not welcomed. In fact having some small amount of self-criticism is good for you because it can act as the much needed reality check to help you develop in to a better person. For example, if you are thinking "I need to shed some weight" then you will be motivated to work out, eat healthy and generally lead a better lifestyle. The problem comes in when you use it excessively by focusing on your failures alone therefore reducing your self-esteem and this can even lead to depression in extreme cases. For example, if you say "I am fat and ugly" which might make you feel bad about yourself.

You might have made the wise decision to use positive affirmations but this doesn't mean you won't have some negative thoughts creeping in to your head once in a while. The important thing is to know how to shut them out in order to continue on your journey of positive thinking and positive results.

1. Put the negative thoughts inside a box

We normally experience both success and failure in life. However, there are times when your mind can turn a minor mistake in to an epic failure which keeps eating at you and brings you down. When you get these negative thoughts, you can take some deep breaths before taking the problems and stuffing them inside the smallest box possible. For example, you might make a mistake during a meeting and instead of making statements such as "I 'm an idiot and I've ruined my career," you can say "I employed poor choice of words." When you think of the small box that this problem should fit in, you close the chapter and do not spread the negative talk to other areas of your life. When this box of problems appears small then you feel confident enough to handle it as opposed to when you make it to be a very big deal.

2. Use positive thinking

When things seem to be going wrong, we are often under pressure to change it all and make them positive. According to research, when you force yourself to make positive affirmations when you are down then you often feel worse. This is due to the fact that the internal lie detector in you goes off.

A technique that is recommended by experts in this case is known as possible thinking. This involves having positive thoughts about the situation at hand and stating the facts. Instead of thinking "I'm a fat cow" you can turn it to be "I would like to shed about 10 pounds." By doing this, you feel like you have many choices and directions to choose from and there is a way out of that situation.

3. Ask yourself whether you are very guilty

There are times when you find yourself blowing things out of proportion and having many unnecessary negative thoughts. For example, if you think you embarrassed yourself in a meeting by saying something inappropriate, you can try to remember if everyone recoiled in horror or if the majority were actually busy on their phones and didn't pay attention to what you did. By doing this, you will be kind to yourself therefore greatly reducing the number of negative thoughts running through your mind. This will be a better way of handling the situation. Your focus should be on making moments less embarrassing or humiliating as opposed to having thought such as "I made a fool of myself" which only bring you down.

4. Name your inner critic

Think of a silly name for your inner critic and by doing this, you will never take that critic seriously and wouldn't let it affect how you view yourself. For example, you might refer to it as "the Nag" which might help to loosen the emotional hold it has over you. In the end, you won't give it much importance.

5. Give things a better spin

Sometimes all you need to do to silence that negative voice inside you is to change your choice of words. For example, if you are panicking about getting things done then you should avoid saying "I am very disorganized, I will never be able to get things done, " you can instead say " I am having a feeling that I won't be able to get this done." This may appear silly but something as simple as this can avoid damaging your self-esteem because you will simply think of it as a moment that will pass as opposed to when you feel like that's you or your life. For example, when thinking of a past embarrassing moment you can say " I felt rather stupid" instead of saying " I am so stupid" the former statement narrows it down to how you felt at that time while the latter one defines who you are.

6. Ask yourself what your best friend would say

This is where it really helps to have great friends who always have something good to say in every situation. For example, if you are beating yourself about a scenario where you thought you humiliated yourself, think about what your best friend would say and this would probably be something like "Oh please, was it that bad?" When you think about it from your friends' perspective then the whole situation won't seem that bad. One rule you have to adhere to when doing this is that, you shouldn't tell yourself something you would never say to your friend. For example, you wouldn't refer to your friend as a "total slob" if he or she drops some food on his or her shirt therefore you should never refer to yourself as one too.

7. Pick up the phone

Have you realized that shame only affects you when you hide it? For example, if you think you made a fool of yourself when with your friends then you can pick up the phone and say something like "I am in a complete shame downward spiral" and then explain why you feel so in a few sentences before laughing. When you do this, you would have removed the shame and you won't have your inner voice bothering you about it. Therefore, it is important to be courageous enough to engage in a counterintuitive act and explain to someone the events that took place. Most of the time, you will end up laughing about them.

8. Embrace your imperfections

Everyone has imperfections from the person you think looks flawless to yourself. There is always something that one would like to change about themselves. Thinking about these imperfections only make you depressed and drag self-esteem downwards. One of the best ways of dealing with this is by embracing your imperfections. One of the ways of reducing stress is by not setting unreasonably high standards for yourself. Although perfectionism can push you to explore your full potential, it can also be very destructive when taken too far. When you hear successful people talk of how they got to where they are, you won't hear them mention that they owe their success to perfectionism. Most of the times, their success comes from their willingness to push on even when faced with failure along the way. This means that it is okay to relax your standards a bit and show yourself the same level of empathy you would give a friend. In this way, you will be able to overcome your inner critic.

Chapter 5: Steps towards achieving positive self-talk

The mind is a very busy place that can be filled thoughts which may be positive or negative. One frightening thing is that most of the self-talk we have is usually negative and this prevents us from going after our hearts' desires. This in turn keeps us from our destiny. This is why more people are paying attention to positive affirmations to try and change this. Altering how we think of ourselves has an impact on the actions we take. With self-talk, you can be able to achieve personal growth in various aspects such as emotional, spiritual, financial and physical. If you have made the decision to start practicing positive self-talk then you need to know the steps you can take to achieve this. The result will be empowering thoughts followed by greater actions.

1. Get rid of your inner critic

If you want to practice positive thinking then you need to get rid of your inner critic that always seems to bring you down. The first step towards achieving this is through awareness. When you dig deep within yourself, you will be surprised at the kinds of emotions buried within you that feed the negative thoughts you carry. When you explore these emotions such as hurt and anger, you will be able to deal with them in order to allow positive thoughts and self-talk.

This is a process that can take a long time and can be difficult especially if you have been engaging in negative thoughts and self-talk for a long time. For example, may be you didn't get something right in first grade and your teacher referred to you as "stupid". If you believed this and thought of yourself as stupid while growing up then this is not something you will get over in a day. This is because your inner voice will keep on reminding you that you are stupid, slow, and fat or any negative way you think of yourself.

A form of negative talk that many people involve themselves in is using the words "I can't." This statement has a huge impact in a negative way and whenever you use it or say that something is too difficult then this builds some kind of resistance which will prevent you from accomplishing the task at hand even if you are very capable of achieving it.

Every time you find yourself using the words "I can't...." you can challenge it by asking yourself, "Why can't I?" According to research, most geniuses achieve what they have through putting in lots of hard work. This means you should start using the words "I can" more than you are currently doing. You can find ways of blocking negative thoughts from your mind whenever you start having them. For example, you can say out loudly "cancel" in order to stop yourself from thinking or making up negative thoughts.

2. Positive affirmations

Repeating positive affirmations will help them embed themselves in your subconscious mind. This in turn leads to more options with regards to new thoughts. What you need to know about repeating affirmations is that it is important to say them out aloud and with emotion. Just reading the words without feeling them or believing them is of no use. Your subconscious mind has the ability to take the orders given by your mouth but only if you do so in total faith and after repeating it. This is why experts stress that you should repeat these affirmations daily.

This might be difficult in the beginning and you may be filled with skepticism when saying your positive affirmations. However, with time, you will believe more and more in your statements which will greatly influence your success.

3. Positive scripts

You may have noticed that it is easier for negative thoughts to pile up once they begin. In addition to this drama piling up, it leads to a lot of drama that can end up trapping and limiting you. You can use this trend to your advantage by starting a series of positive thoughts that can run similar to a movie script. It can be more effective if you add some visualization to it. If you tell yourself a story about achieving your goals for a long period of time then you will start to believe it. You will be able to internalize these goals and dreams which will push you to achieve them.

4. Replace the negative thoughts you have with positive ones

There are some external factors that may influence the thoughts you have and you need to identify these factors. For example, you can find yourself spending lots of time with friends who are toxic and their negative thoughts may rub off on you if you are not careful. This means you should be careful with the kind of negative influences around you. If these negative thoughts originate from your friends then you can choose to limit the amount of time you spend with them. If the people you expose yourself to do not support your dreams and goals, it is advisable to have people who are able to empower you and their positive thoughts and actions will rub off on you.

This will make you feel more motivated to pursue greater self growth. Your self-talk will be influenced by the positive energy radiating from them.

5. Present tense messages

We all have goals which we would like to achieve and this doesn't mean it is easy to do that. There are steps you need to take in order to achieve these goals. The entire process can end up becoming stressful when you dwell on it too much. What you can do to prevent this is to focus on the steps you are able to make presently to move you closer to your goals. There are times you may be stuck and seem to see no way forward. When this happens and you are thinking "What can I do right now?"You can change this trail of thought from being anxious about the future to thinking about what you can manage to do in the present. You have to know that future occurrences may be out of your control but you can do something today that might create favorable effects in future. In order for you to take the necessary steps towards achieving these actions, you need to concentrate on your inner talk which should be positive.

6. Confront your fears

There are many things that may hinder your path to success and the greatest one of them is fear. The reason people get scared of taking chances is due to the fact that they fear losing the security they are currently enjoy. When faced with a choice of taking a chance at pursuing your dreams, you may be crippled by fear and therefore seek to talk yourself into believing that you are happy and fine with your current state even if that is not the case. Even if you try to lie to yourself by making false positive self-talk, your inner self knows the truth.

Now that we have established the importance of confronting your fears, you should ask yourself what your fears are. The next thing you should think about is the worst thing that can happen. When you approach your fear step by step then you are able to break it down. This will enable you find a positive way of viewing things thereby increasing your chances of succeeding. In fact, when you finally confront your fears, you will realize that the situation wasn't as bad as you feared. Actually, the benefits you enjoy from making this change will be worth the risk. Your positive inner talk will be responsible for effecting change.

7. Concentrate on enjoyable moments

Having a positive attitude comes much easier when you concentrate on the great moments that life gives you instead of only dwelling on the difficult ones which may end up depressing you. You have to be prepared for the fact that you will encounter challenges since they are part of life. However, consider that although there are downs in life, there are some ups too and these are what you should focus on to help make it through the bad times.

You can make the decision to have positive thoughts coupled with positive affirmations and make it a habit to do this. Whenever you find your mind wandering on the negative side, find a way to turn that around to the positive. A great way of starting this journey is by being grateful for the things you currently have in your life. Your mind will benefit a lot from gratitude and in turn the self-talk you engage in will begin to create change and bring you joy.

8. Develop psychological distance from yourself

When you are feeling stressed or anxious, it is important to stop using the first person phase at times. For example, instead of asking yourself "Why am I so stressed?" you can choose to use your name or come up with a second name that you can use when addressing such situations. The question you can ask yourself in this case is "Why are you feeling stressed?" This is a great way of developing psychological distance between yourself and the circumstance at hand. This will reduce the amount of discomfort you are feeling and the pressure that comes with it. You will then view the situation as an interesting challenge as opposed to a threat.

9. Don't be hard on yourself

When you face some failures or difficulties in life, you might find yourself thinking negatively which may only increase your level of stress. This may prevent you from reaching your potential. Instead, you should not be so hard on yourself. Apply the same compassion you would use on a friend or someone you hold dear. If you feel like saying negative things such as "I am terrible at this" change it to "Relax, you can do this."

Final thoughts

The power of positive self-talk cannot be overemphasized due to the great benefits it holds such as the ability to actually make one pursue his or her dreams and goals. However, this is not always an easy process especially due to the fact that there are lots of negative thoughts and talk that always want to triumph over the positive ones. Therefore, you should not think this is a process that will happen overnight. If your mind was previously filled with negative thoughts then you need to be prepared for the time and effort it will take to turn this around.

By following the tips provided in this book, you will be in a good position to actually experience a tremendous improvement in your life. There are many people who talk themselves down and this makes it difficult to accomplish the goals they have in life. If you are one of them then do not despair because there is hope and you can follow the steps outlined in this book to be able to get out of this predicament.

Although the journey towards positive affirmation may be challenging, the results are quite rewarding and you will experience a higher level of happiness and peace. Above everything else, you will feel more empowered. Positive affirmations may be the push you require to move in the right direction and achieve success.